W9-AKX-299

NO LEV 12/12

J   11.95   153717
921.   PT.0191.89.01
CAESAR, JULIUS
JULIUS CAESAR BY
MATTHEWS

PEACHTREE CITY LIBRARY
201 Willowbend Road
Peachtree City, GA 30269

FLINT RIVER REGIONAL LIBRARY

Peachtree City Library
201 Willowbend Road
Peachtree City, Ga. 30269

Julius Caesar

Rupert Matthews

Illustrations by Doug Post

The Bookwright Press
New York · 1989

FLINT RIVER REGIONAL LIBRARY

Great Lives

Beethoven
Louis Braille
Julius Caesar
Winston Churchill
Captain Cook
Marie Curie
Charles Dickens
Francis Drake
Einstein
Queen Elizabeth I
Queen Elizabeth II
Anne Frank
Gandhi
Henry VIII
Helen Keller

Joan of Arc
John F. Kennedy
Martin Luther King, Jr.
John Lennon
Ferdinand Magellan
Karl Marx
Mary, Queen of Scots
Mozart
Napoleon
Florence Nightingale
Elvis Presley
William Shakespeare
Mother Teresa
Tchaikovsky
Queen Victoria

Title page: An ancient statue of Caesar, showing him wearing the equipment and armor of a senior army officer.

First published in the
United States in 1989 by
The Bookwright Press
387 Park Avenue, South
New York, NY 10016

First published in 1988 by
Wayland (Publishers) Ltd
61 Western Road, Hove
East Sussex BN3 1JD, England

© Copyright 1988 Wayland (Publishers) Limited

Picture credits
Michael Holford 22, 25, 29; The
Mansell Collection 16, 18; Ronald
Sheridan's Photo-Library *title page*,
5, 11, 12, 20 (left); Wayland Picture
Library 20 (top), 28.

Library of Congress Cataloging-in-Publication Data

Matthews, Rupert
    Julius Caesar/by Rupert Matthews: illustrations
by Douglas Post.
        p.   cm. – (Great lives)
    Bibliography: p.
    Includes index.
    Summary: A biography of the Roman general and
statesman whose brilliant military leadership
helped make Rome the center of a vast empire.
    ISBN 0–531–18243–6
    1. Caesar, Julius – Juvenile literature.   2. Rome –
History-Republic, 265–30 B.C. – Juvenile literature.
3. Heads of state – Rome – Biography – Juvenile
literature. 4. Generals – Rome – Biography –
Juvenile literature.
[1. Caesar, Julius.   2. Heads of state.   3. Generals.
4. Rome – History – Republic, 265–30 B.C.]
I. Post, Doug.   ill.   II. Title.   III. Series: Great lives
(New York, N.Y.)
DG261.M35 1989   88–19880
937'.05'0924 – dc 19   CIP
[B]   AC

Phototypeset by Kalligraphics Ltd, Redhill, Surrey,
England
Printed in Italy by G. Canale C.S.p.A., Turin

Contents

Hail Caesar!

Gaius Julius Caesar was one of the greatest men of the ancient world. He led Roman armies to victory over foreign enemies and extended the Roman Empire to include vast new territories. These achievements brought wealth and glory to Rome.

When civil war broke out in Rome, Caesar led his armies against the best troops and generals in the world. From these numerous campaigns and battles, Caesar and his armies emerged victorious. By the end of his life, Caesar had become the undisputed leader of Rome and had begun to introduce important reforms.

The supporters of Julius Caesar believed him to be a politician of superb ability who could right the many wrongs that existed in Roman society. However, some of his colleagues felt that Caesar was an unscrupulous and arrogant dictator. Rather than allow themselves to be ruled by such a man, they murdered Caesar.

Both these views of Julius Caesar are partly correct. He was a clever politician and general who achieved much good. But he was also an unscrupulous and ruthless ruler.

The successes of Julius Caesar dazzled his contemporaries. Even today they seem astounding. He has the reputation of having been a great man, and the facts about his life bear this out. The story of Julius Caesar is one of the most brilliant of the ancient world.

Left *Caesar riding through the streets of Rome in triumph.*

Right *A relief showing a Roman soldier fighting a Celtic warrior.*

A Roman childhood

Gaius Julius Caesar was born in Rome on July 12, 102 BC. His father, also named Gaius Julius Caesar, was a member of one of the noblest patrician families in Rome. The Caesars claimed to trace their ancestry back to the goddess Venus. However, despite this, the family was far from wealthy.

As the son of an important family, Caesar received a good education. He learned how to read and write and studied such subjects as history, philosophy and arithmetic. Because it was usual for patricians to have a career in politics or the army, Caesar was also taught the art of public speaking, or rhetoric.

A patrician makes a speech in the Senate.

The fact that Caesar's family were patricians was enormously important for his future career. Rome's society and political organization were built upon a rigid class structure. At the top of Roman society were the patrician families, like Caesar's. Only patricians were allowed to sit in the Senate, the group of people that decided government policy, or were permitted to become consuls, the most important political job in Rome.

Left *A Roman schoolroom. Many teachers were highly educated Greek slaves.*

Below the patricians were the equites. These families were often very rich, but had little political power. Most Roman citizens were plebeians. These were the ordinary citizens of Rome. Plebeians could vote to accept or reject the policies of the Senate.

By the time of Caesar, the population of Rome also included thousands of people who were not Roman citizens at all. These might be slaves captured during wars, or freemen from other countries. These people were not allowed to vote and had no political power.

7

Captured by pirates

When Caesar was 15 years old his father died. Almost at once Caesar entered a career in public service. Through friends of the family, Caesar obtained a minor diplomatic post and then served for a time in the army.

In 76 BC, Julius Caesar decided to travel to Rhodes, a Greek island in the Mediterranean Sea, to study under the famous Greek orator Apollonius Molon. Caesar

hoped to improve his public speaking skills in order to help his career. At this time Caesar was 26 years old.

As Caesar was sailing to Rhodes, the ship on which he was traveling was captured by pirates. The pirates realized that Caesar was a nobleman and decided to get a ransom for him.

The pirate chief set the price of Caesar's freedom at 20 talents. This was a huge amount of money, equivalent to many times the average yearly wage.

However, Caesar laughed. He told the pirates he was worth at least 50 talents and then added that he would one day execute them all. This time it was the pirates' turn to laugh. They could not imagine how such a young man could possibly hurt them. Local Roman officials paid the ransom and Caesar was released.

Caesar at once took action. Although he had no official authority, Caesar took charge of several warships and put to sea. He tracked down the pirates and captured them. True to his word, Caesar then executed them all. The incident was not particularly important outside the local area, but it added greatly to Caesar's reputation in Rome. People now thought of him as a man of action and determination.

Left *Caesar is threatened by the pirate captain. At this time piracy was a serious menace to shipping. It was not until many years after the time of Caesar that piracy was stamped out by the Roman navy.*

Early politics

In 73 BC, Caesar returned to Rome and reentered politics. Again through family influence, Caesar became a priest. This post enabled him to mix with important people and to become involved with affairs of state.

Caesar made friends quickly and easily. One of these new acquaintances was a Senator called Marcus Licinius Crassus. Crassus was the wealthiest man in Rome. He had made his fortune from buying and selling property.

In 65 BC, Caesar obtained the post of *Curule Aedile*. As *Curule*, Caesar was responsible for maintaining public buildings

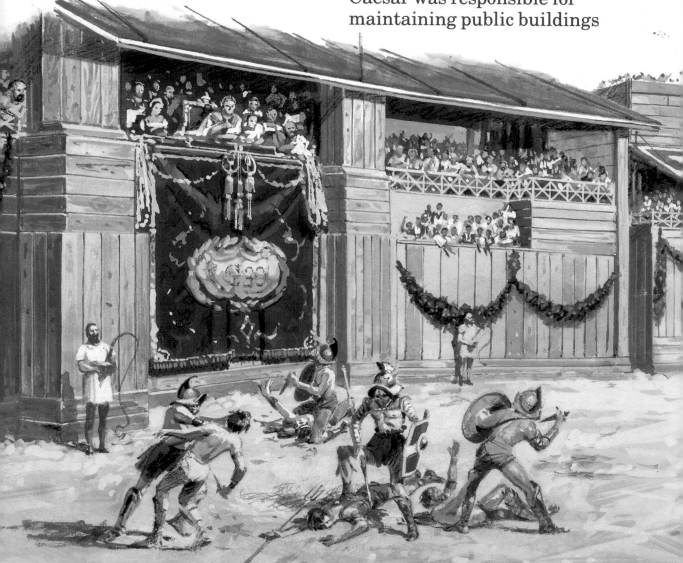

within Rome and organizing festivals. Caesar saw this as an opportunity to win popularity with the plebeians. He borrowed a large amount of money from Crassus and spent it all providing entertainments for the citizens of Rome.

Right *A terracotta statue of gladiators. Gladiators were great sporting heroes, just as football players are today.*

Religious festivals were celebrated in a style never before seen. Caesar also organized spectacular gladiatorial fights. In one day, 640 gladiators, equipped with silver armor, butchered each other for the entertainment of the crowd. These shows won Caesar great popularity with the ordinary citizens.

Caesar next made use of Crassus' money to bribe his way into the job of Chief Priest, despite the fact that he did not believe in the gods and goddesses of ancient Rome. He wanted the position because it had many political advantages.

Left *Gladiators fought in wooden arenas before huge crowds.*

The Triumvirate

In 61 BC Caesar was granted the governorship of the province of Farther Spain. He was away for a year, during which time he fought successfully against mountain bandits. He gained the reputation of being an outstanding soldier. When Caesar returned to Rome he found that he was in a good position from which to improve his career.

Gnaeus Pompey, a famous general who had won many victories in the eastern Mediterranean, had returned to Rome. However, the Senate refused to accept the peace terms Pompey had made with eastern rulers. The Senate also refused to give the customary presents of farms to Pompey's old and experienced soldiers. Pompey was furious.

When Caesar arrived in Rome, he offered to help by arranging a deal between Crassus and Pompey. By acting as a go-between, Caesar was able to further his own career.

The three men agreed that Caesar should become one of the two consuls for the year 59 BC. As consul, Caesar would be able to arrange laws favorable to both Crassus and Pompey. The agreement among the three powerful men became known as the Triumvirate.

During the consular elections, which were held soon after, Crassus bribed many people, and Pompey used the influence of his ex-soldiers to help Caesar to become consul.

Left *This coin (enlarged view) bears the image of Pompey and was used by him to pay his soldiers. The bust of Pompey is surrounded by laurels, the symbol of victory. The coin was designed to remind everyone that Pompey was a great general.*

Caesar, Pompey and Crassus secretly decided government policy and appointments that were to their own advantage.

As the most important official in Rome, Caesar was able to help his friends. He granted farms to Pompey's soldiers and drew up new tax laws that added to the already immense fortune of Crassus. Some of these measures were illegal, but nobody dared oppose the powerful Triumvirate. Caesar also made several useful reforms concerning the administration of the Empire, but only those measures that would not offend his partners in the Triumvirate.

The conquest of Gaul

After a year in office each consul was entitled to become Governor of a province. Consuls usually chose the wealthiest province available so that they could make large amounts of money.

Through the influence of the Triumvirate, Caesar obtained three provinces: those of Illyricum, Cisalpine Gaul and Transalpine Gaul. These provinces covered most of northern Italy and the southern coast of modern France.

Stationed within the provinces was a large army, of which Caesar became commander-in-chief. Knowing that he would need to rely on the soldiers, Caesar took great care of them.

Below *Caesar leads his troops against the Gauls. These battles were ferocious and hard-fought. Thousands of men were killed during the conquest of Gaul.*

He made sure that they were paid on time and always had enough food. He also trained the men to perfection. At the same time, Caesar introduced many reforms that helped the civilians within his provinces. This earned him many friends.

North of the coastal strip held by Rome, Gaul was divided among a large number of warlike and ferocious tribes. In a brilliant two-year campaign, Caesar completely defeated these tribes. He brought the fertile and wealthy lands of Gaul under the control of the Roman Empire.

Caesar made sure that the people in Rome heard about his great achievements. He sent regular messages to Rome giving news of his brilliant conquests. In 55 BC two tribes rebelled against Roman control. Caesar at once defeated them in battle and then killed them all.

In 52 BC a more widespread revolt broke out under the command of the Gallic hero Vercingetorix. After a hard campaign, Caesar defeated the Gauls and sent Vercingetorix to Rome as a prisoner. Caesar was determined to show the Romans that he was a great general.

The invasion of Britain

As soon as he had finished his first conquest of Gaul, Caesar turned his eyes farther north. Across the sea, he knew, lay the islands of Britain. Caesar had heard that they were very rich in minerals. If he could extend his power to Britain, he would increase his reputation for glory still further.

A stone carving of a Roman bireme – a type of warship.

In the summer of 55 BC, Caesar set sail. The expedition was not a success. Part of the invasion fleet lost its way during the sea crossing, and those troops who did arrive were daunted by the large British army waiting on the beaches. While Caesar was wondering what to do next, the standard bearer of the X legion leaped from his ship into the surf. Rather than see their eagle standard fall into enemy hands,

the legionaries followed the standard bearer and stormed ashore. After a fierce battle the Romans were able to land.

But several misfortunes occurred. First, a detachment of troops was ambushed. A great storm then blew up and wrecked many ships. Caesar was forced to retreat less than three weeks after arriving.

The following year Caesar returned with a bigger army and fleet. This time he defeated a large British army. However, he failed to find a safe harbor for his ships and they were again wrecked by a storm. After forcing several British tribes to pay tribute (tax), Caesar had to retreat once more.

Although he had not succeeded in conquering Britain, Caesar turned the events to political advantage. In his writings, *The Gallic Wars*, Caesar presented his raids on Britain as great victories and scarcely mentioned his failures. Caesar was continually concerned about his popularity in Rome. He had good reason to worry.

Caesar kept a careful note of everything that happened and sent regular messages to Rome.

Crossing the Rubicon

A bust of Marcus Tullius Cicero, one of the politicians who opposed Caesar's dictatorial powers.

While Caesar was busy in Gaul and Britain, political events in Rome moved quickly. Many senators resented the power held by the Triumvirate. They wanted a return to the system of government under which the Senate held power.

Two of the most important of the senators opposed to the Triumvirate were Cato and Cicero. They decided to try to disrupt the unity of the Triumvirate. Pompey had remained in Rome, so the senators tried to win him over by persuasion. Rumors were spread suggesting that Caesar was becoming too powerful, and Pompey became jealous. However, messengers sent by Caesar, and the efforts of Crassus, held the Triumvirate together. But in 53 BC Crassus was killed in battle.

Within a few more years, Pompey had been won over by Cicero and Cato. Although Caesar had achieved great glory, his position suddenly became unsafe.

Right *Roman legions awaiting Caesar's decision to cross the Rubicon.*

The senators produced evidence that Caesar had acted illegally while consul. As soon as Caesar ceased to be Governor they could prosecute him. Pompey took the side of the Senate and was given wide-ranging powers.

Caesar was faced by a terrible decision. If he stayed in his provinces, his governorship would end and he would be arrested, and possibly executed, as a criminal. If on the other hand he marched on Rome, he would become a rebel and a traitor. Hoping to avoid either fate, Caesar sent his trusted friend Mark Antony to Rome, suggesting a compromise that would ensure his own safety. But Pompey and the consuls refused.

On the night of January 10, 49 BC, Caesar marched his troops to the Rubicon River. This stream marked the boundary between Caesar's provinces and Italy. Once he crossed the Rubicon, Caesar knew, civil war was inevitable. Caesar stopped and gazed thoughtfully at the Rubicon. Then he declared, "Let the die be cast," and crossed the river.

The defeat of Pompey

After crossing the Rubicon, Caesar marched to Rome. Most of the legions stationed in Italy were loyal to Caesar and they flocked to join him. Pompey and the Republican senators sailed for Greece, where their troops were stationed.

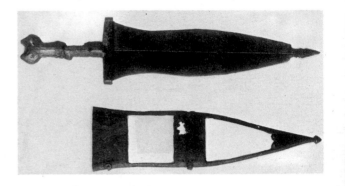

A Roman legionary's iron dagger and dagger sheath.

Caesar spent several months in Italy raising money and preparing for the war against Pompey. Some of Caesar's actions, such as plundering the treasury in Rome, made him unpopular in the city. But he needed the money to pay his troops.

In the summer, Caesar marched to Spain and defeated the Roman army stationed there, an army that was loyal to Pompey. Returning to Rome, Caesar had himself elected consul. Then, in the spring of 48 BC, he sailed on to Greece.

Left *The tombstone of a Roman centurion. He holds in his hand the eagle standard of his legion.*

For several months the armies of Caesar and Pompey marched across Greece, both commanders trying to gain an advantage. Eventually, the two armies met on August 9 on the Plain of Pharsalus. Though outnumbered by about two to one, Caesar's troops outflanked those of Pompey and utterly defeated them. Pompey's army lost 15,000 dead and 20,000 captured. Only a few hundred escaped.

The fighting at Pharsalus was long and bitter, but ended with victory for Caesar.

Caesar knew that the deaths of so many Romans might lose him supporters. As he gazed upon the bodies he declared, "they asked for it." Caesar later tried hard to justify his actions.

Among those who escaped from Pharsalus was Pompey. He fled to Egypt where he had many friends.

Caesar in Egypt

After his great victory at Pharsalus, Caesar was prevented from chasing Pompey by other, more pressing needs. He was very short of money to pay his troops. Caesar also needed to buy stores and provisions. He therefore set about raising cash.

Caesar forced several of the richest cities in the region to give him money. He also raised funds by promising to reduce future tax bills in return for an immediate payment. With his cash problems solved, Caesar started in pursuit of Pompey.

On October 2, 48 BC, Caesar arrived at Alexandria in Egypt.

Part of a Roman mosaic from the time of Caesar showing the Nile delta in Egypt.

The Egyptians sent messengers out to meet him. One of them carried Pompey's severed head. Caesar was horrified. He had not wanted to kill his old friend, but merely to strip him of power.

At this time Egypt was ruled by the Pharaoh Ptolemy XIII and his sister Cleopatra VII. The two rulers hated each other, and the country was on the brink of civil war. In an attempt to gain the throne for herself, Cleopatra arranged a meeting with Caesar.

It is said that she had herself wrapped in a carpet, which was then given to Caesar as a gift.

Soon Caesar became involved in a love affair with Cleopatra. He took her side in the dispute and deposed Ptolemy.

Below *Caesar was greatly impressed by Egypt's enormous wealth.*

While Caesar stayed in Egypt, his enemies were gathering fresh armies. In the autumn of 47 BC and the following spring, Caesar defeated these armies in three lightning campaigns. One of these was so swift that Caesar was able to describe it in perhaps his most famous words, *"Veni, Vidi, Vici,"* which mean "I came, I saw, I conquered."

Dictator of Rome

As Dictator, Caesar could issue new laws and decrees that nobody dared oppose.

On his return to Rome, after the Battle of Munda, which brought the civil war to an end, Caesar was declared Dictator of Rome. This position carried far-reaching and tyrannical powers, yet was not against the law. On many previous occasions in Roman history, men had been created Dictator. However, these appointments had been for a short period of time only. Caesar was made Dictator for life.

Using his new powers, Caesar began to reorganize the system of government. The Senate was enlarged to include 900 members, drawn from many walks of life.

At the same time it was stripped of most of its strength. The power to declare war, for instance, was transferred from the Senate to the Dictator. These measures had the effect of taking government control away from the patricians.

The long-established position of consul also suffered a loss of dignity and power. On one occasion, Caesar did not allow consular elections to take place at all. Financial control of the Empire was brought under much tighter supervision than before. Caesar took control of the treasury and began to coin money bearing his likeness.

Caesar greatly improved the lives of the plebeians by protecting their jobs from being taken over by slave labor. The massive building programs begun by Caesar also gave work and security to the ordinary citizens of Rome.

Caesar's reforms were undoubtedly much needed, but his motives for making them are not clear. Though his actions greatly aided the government of Rome, they also had the effect of establishing his dictatorship more securely. We cannot be sure whether he was acting in self-interest or out of a genuine desire for improvement.

Below *Chariot racing was one of the entertainments organized by Caesar to win favor with the plebeians.*

The murder of Caesar

A. By the year 44 BC, Caesar was firmly established as the supreme power in Rome. He had carefully removed any real authority from other officials and had concentrated all political power in his own hands.

Caesar had not used this power selfishly. His many reforms had been much needed. Rome was better governed than it had been for many years. These actions earned him many friends in the provinces and among the equites and plebeians in Rome. However, Caesar had become increasingly unpopular with the patricians, who had previously been in sole charge of the government of Rome. Caesar was soon to alienate them even further and anger the ordinary citizens too.

The people of Rome were greatly attached to their Republican system of government. They considered it far superior to that of any kingdom. In 44 BC, Caesar declared that after his death the dictatorship would pass on to his nephew, Octavian. Most Romans welcomed Caesar's dictatorship, but did not want it to become hereditary.

In March, Caesar called a meeting of the Senate. It had become clear that the nations of the eastern Mediterranean would respect Caesar if he was a king far more than as a dictator. Caesar therefore wanted the Senate to give him a royal title.

One group of senators found this idea totally unacceptable. Prominent among these men were Brutus, Cassius and Casca, who had previously been associates of Caesar. They wanted a return to the Republic that had governed Rome before Caesar took power. Caesar arrived at the Senate on March 15 (known as the Ides of March). As he entered the building, the conspirators leaped at him and stabbed him to death. Caesar fell at the base of a statue of Pompey, his old rival.

Right *Caesar was stabbed 23 times and died almost at once. After the attack everyone fled the scene, except three slaves who carried Caesar's body home.*

Caesar's legacy

After the murder of Caesar, Rome was plunged into chaos. The conspirators, with the aid of Cicero, persuaded the Senate to abolish the dictatorship and attempted to restore the Republic. However, Mark Antony and Octavian opposed a return to government by the patricians.

They gained the support of the plebeians and of a large section of the army.

Within a few months, the political situation had broken down completely. Civil war broke out between the conspirators and Antony and Octavian. By the end of 42 BC the conspirators had been defeated. Nine years later, Octavian and Antony quarreled. Antony was defeated in the war that followed, and Octavian became the master of the Roman Empire.

Octavian took the name Augustus, by which he is best known, and began to make his position stronger. Although he followed Caesar's lead in many things, Augustus never tried to become king or to overthrow the Senate. He remained content to control the government from behind the scenes. In this way, Augustus stayed in power until his death in AD 14.

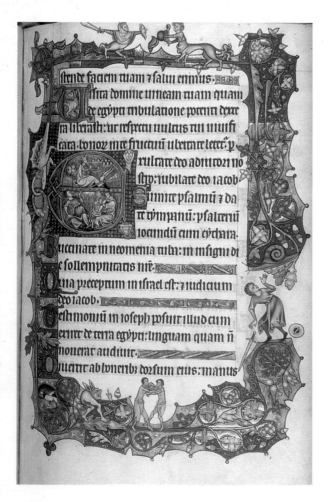

Left *Caesar's conquest of Gaul made the Roman Empire European in outlook. Latin continued to be used by European scholars for many centuries, as shown by this medieval manuscript.*

The career of Caesar was one of the most remarkable in history. He rose from the position of an impoverished noble to be the undisputed master of the mighty Roman Empire. Nor did Caesar's achievements die with him. The government reforms he introduced remained the basis of Roman administration for centuries. By destroying the old Republic, Caesar had laid the foundations of the government by emperors, which would follow and continue until the end of the Roman Empire.

Equally important for future years, was the conquest of Gaul. By taking Roman armies into

The solid Roman buildings remained in use long after the collapse of the Empire in the fifth century. This Roman bridge in Cordoba, Spain, is still in use after some 2,000 years.

northern Europe, Caesar had made Rome far more than a Mediterranean power. Europe was dominated by Rome. The move ensured that learning and literature in Europe would be dominated by Roman ideas for centuries to come. After the fall of the Roman Empire, Europeans looked back to the days of Rome with longing. Even today, the ideas of ancient Rome live on.

Important events

102 BC	(July 12) Gaius Julius Caesar born in Rome.	
87 BC	He enters a political career following the death of his father.	
76 BC	He is captured by pirates in the Mediterranean Sea.	
73 BC	Caesar becomes a priest.	
65 BC	He attains the office of Curule Aedile	
61 BC	Caesar becomes Governor of Farther Spain.	
60 BC	The Triumvirate is formed by Caesar, Crassus and Pompey.	
59 BC	Caesar's year as consul.	

58 BC	Governorship of Illyricum, Cisalpine Gaul and Transalpine Gaul begins.
56 BC	Conquest of Gaul completed.
55 BC	First raid on Britain.
49 BC	Caesar crosses the Rubicon and starts the civil war.
48 BC	Pompey is defeated at the Battle of Pharsalus.
48 BC	Caesar meets Cleopatra.
45 BC	The Battle of Munda ends the civil war.
44 BC	Caesar becomes Dictator for life.
44 BC	(March 15) Caesar murdered.

Books to read

Ancient Rome by Charles Alexander Robinson, Jr. (Franklin Watts, 1984)
Imperial Rome by Jill Hughes (Gloucester Press, 1985)
Julius Caesar and the Romans by Robin May (Bookwright Press, 1985)
The Roman World by Mike Corbishley (Franklin Watts, 1987)
See Inside a Roman Town by Jonathan Rutland (Warwick Press, 1986)

Glossary

Cisalpine Gaul   The area of Gaul between the Alps and the Apennines.

Civilians   People who are not members of the armed forces.

Consul   One of two men, elected annually, who were the most important officials in ancient Rome.

Curule Aedile   The government official responsible for public buildings and entertainments in ancient Rome.

Dictator   A ruler with absolute power over his country and people.

Diplomatic   The branch of the civil service concerned with meeting foreign governments.

Equite   A member of the business or middle class of ancient Rome.

Farther Spain   The area roughly equivalent to modern Portugal and northwest Spain.

Gallic   Relating to Gaul.

Gaul   The territory roughly equivalent to modern France that was inhabited by numerous warlike tribes of Gauls.

Gladiator   A slave or prisoner trained to fight for the amusement of the citizens of Rome and provincial cities.

Hereditary   Inherited from ancestors.

Illyricum   The region that is now part of Yugoslavia and Albania.

Infantrymen   Foot soldiers.

Legion   The most important formation in the Roman army. Each legion consisted of between 3,000 and 6,000 heavily armed infantrymen.

Legionary   A soldier serving in a legion.

Orator   An eloquent public speaker.

Patrician   A member of the nobility of ancient Rome.

Pharaoh   The title of the king of Egypt in ancient times.

Plebeian   A member of the working class of ancient Rome.

Prosecute   To bring legal proceedings against a person.

Ransom   A sum of money paid to obtain the release of a prisoner.

Republic   A form of government without a head of state (such as a king, queen or emperor).

Rhetoric   The art of public speaking.

Senate   The body of men in ancient Rome who collectively ran the government and decided policy.

Senator   A member of the Senate.

Standard bearer   The soldier who carried the sacred eagle standard of the Romans in a battle.

Transalpine Gaul   The area of Gaul northwest of the Alps.

Treasury   The government department in charge of public finance.

Venus   The Roman goddess of love, from whom the family of Julius Caesar claimed descent.

Index

Peachtree City Library
201 Willowbend Road
Peachtree City, Ga. 30269